The Pain We Call Love

By

Joanne Sherry Mitchell

©2024 Joanne Sherry Mitchell. All rights reserved
Including the right to reproduce this book or
Portions thereof in any form whatsoever,
Without permission in writing from the publisher.
Printed in the United States of America.

BOOKS BY JOANNE SHERRY MITCHELL

Moments
Moments And Then Some
Moments When Night Becomes Day
Moments Gentle Hints to Life
Moments Not Things
Moments No Replacement Found
Moments With Mrs. Melissa Sherry Smith 5th Grade Class
Moments Treasured
Momentos De Risa, Dolor y Amor
Moments As Milestones
Πολύτιμες Στιγμές
The Pain We Call Love

Visit Joanne Mitchell's website

www.momentsbyjoanne.com

You may email her

At

moments@momentsbyjoanne.com

ACKNOWLEDGEMENTS

Cover Art by artist Amanda Clark

Cover design edits by Victor Morales, Art Director Professional Management, Inc.

With special thanks for their assistance in bringing to completion this book The Pain We Call Love to:

Betty Smith
Marie Bartlett

A special recognition to **AMANDA CLARK**, a North Carolina Artist, who illustrated the following poems

Lonely Bed	page 10
Keepsakes	page 25
Shook By Drive-By	page 31
Trash	page 43
It's Death	page 50
Chastity	page 56
Young Boy Loved His Grandmother	page 64
Before You Leave	page 79
Weeping	page 92
We Have Grown Old	page 100
Each Month	page 117
Emergency	page 128

Dedicated to my brothers
Chris Sherry, John Sherry, Alex Sherry
For the love that was not pained

Contents

Where Is Love Residing .... page 1
A Whore .... page 2
Mad, Heartbroken and Confused .... page 4
Fate's Hand Holding .... page 5
Doctor's Advice "Cut It Out" .... page 6
My Flower .... page 8
Scorches .... page 9
Lonely Bed .... page 11
Forgiveness .... page 12
My Son The Addict .... page 13
Betrayal .... page 14
Tonight, The Mouth Is Shut .... page 16
A Silent Complainer .... page 17
I Cried .... page 18
Grandma .... page 19
No Impact .... page 20
If You Do Not Keep Me .... page 21
Last Night .... page 22
Upset .... page 23
Keepsakes .... page 24
Like Love .... page 27
I Eat For A Reason .... page 28
Unforgiving .... page 29
Shook By Drive-By .... page 30
How Do You Know .... page 32
Silent .... page 32
We Thought .... page 33
Alcohol .... page 34
Did Not Get One .... page 36
What Is This Burden .... page 38
Enough .... page 39
Arrival .... page 40
The Perfect Alignment .... page 41
Trash .... page 42
Darkness .... page 44
Speaking .... page 45

Annoyances	page 46
Stunned	page 48
Give From God	page 49
It is Death	page 51
Sunrise Calls To Me	page 52
Speak Loud	page 52
My Love	page 53
It Is Done and Over	page 54
Scent of Smoke Remains	page 55
Chastity	page 56
Once We Were Thought of As Us	page 57
You're Married	page 58
The Strength of Two	page 59
My Wife Was Never Interested In Being Faithful	page 60
She Said I Love You	page 61
Haunted	page 62
Stupid	page 63
Young Boy Loved His Grandmother	page 65
Isolation	page 66
Her Forgiveness	page 68
Teenager At Risk	page 70
Granddaughter Not Having Fun	page 72
Letting Myself Die	page 74
It Seems We Hurry Love	page 76
The Momentary Pleasure	page 77
Mistakes Are Made	page 78
Before You Leave	page 79
Always	page 80
The Essence Of Longing	page 82
The Purple Bruise	page 83
At Death	page 84
I Wanted Solitude	page 86
I Want To Dance	page 87
Wrote A Letter To Mom	page 88
Need To Separate	page 89
She And I Are In Love	page 90
Weeping	page 93
Goodbye My Love	page 94

He Has Grown Cold	page 95
Ongoing Adversity	page 96
Show Me	page 97
Talking Backwards	page 98
We Have Grown Old	page 101
Years Ago	page 102
Love Together	page 104
He Is Dead	page 105
Married Thirty-Seven Years	page 106
Love Corroded	page 107
Smart Crazy	page 108
Morning Saddens Wakes One	page 110
Listen	page 111
My Unheard Story	page 112
This Is Love	page 113
One More	page 114
Each Month	page 116
I fell In Love	page 118
Shy Of Forecast	page 119
I Recruited	page 120
Absence Of Wonder	page 121
Wronged By Love	page 122
Sadness	page 123
Anonymity	page 124
No Battle Today	page 125
Protection	page 126
It's A Loss	page 127
Emergency	page 128
I Watched Others	page 130
Love's High Stake	page 131
While I Cry	page 132
My Loss	page 133
Stupidity	page 134
Bittersweet	page 136
I Want to Call It A Thing	page 138
Wept	page 140
Every Time	page 141

There is no equal to

Love

We endure pain

For love

With hope

Love

is brighter

Than the pain is darker

WHERE IS LOVE RESIDING

Within my heart

Under the bed

My bank account

Does it even reside

Close enough for touch?

Love is at play

Playing hide and seek

Come find me,

I hear the echoes of love

Come find me.

I never liked being 'it'

The seeker

I liked being sought.

Now, my mind

Is caught

In the mist

Of a hunt

Above all, I want to find

Where love resides.

Love has become

A need

For this lonely soul.

A WHORE

I did not call her that

She told me

When I asked her

How come you have so many boyfriends?

Honey, she said

I am a whore.

I enjoy the activity

Of which I get paid

These businessmen

Especially married men and

Women

Who prefer women.

It's exciting, a bit dangerous

It's opportunity

To travel, meet all kinds

Of interesting people

The danger that comes

The occasional nutcase

The ones that cannot control their

Substance abuse, tempers, or losses.

At the beginning the money was not good

My regulars stayed with me

They made more; I made more

Gifts I received got better too.

I did have to give up family, marriage, love

Their boundaries did not match mine.

When she stops the story

I look out the window

Wondering

How hard the wind is blowing

On this dark and dreary day.

Who makes all the right choices?

MAD, HEARTBROKEN AND CONFUSED

The disorder I now live with

I was so mad at mom for leaving dad

They seemed happy

I with my own eyes have seen them

Hold hands, kiss each other

Hug after their dinner parties.

How can they break up our family?

Heartbroken because now I

Realize love is not forever

It's good until it's over.

I lost my home

Now I have to choose

Do I go with mom or dad?

Confusing since I do not want either;

Confused since they both want me.

FATE'S HAND HOLDING

For the quick kiss before he left for the office

Somehow I knew, it would be the last

I got up from my chair with happy tears

I loved this man

So I ran after him, for one last hug, and

A second kiss upon my thinning hair.

Unable to recall our last conversation

Yet, having the ability to recall our last kiss.

DOCTOR'S ADVISE "CUT IT OUT"

You have to have

A hysterectomy

No husband

No kids yet

My choice.

Now

My breast will never

Know the comfort

Of feeding a child

The female parts did

Not do what they were created

To do.

You can wait for the cancer

To spread from

Its present location

Cancer soon visits

Stomach, kidney, colon.

Female parts did some good

They helped develop

Breast and hips.

Besides

No one is dead

It's the knife that will bring

Death

Of what might have been.

MY FLOWER

Cannot decide

Not to bloom

My flower

Is destined to bloom

Then

Quietly fall

To the ground

When the bloom has

Lived its life.

SCORCHES

I'm lying on the beach

Hot sand, bright sun

I need the pain

On my skin

Being

Scorched by the sun

I allow this

For need

My broken heart

Did not deliver enough

Pain

I asked the sun

For help

LONELY BED

No matter how close we make love

This bed is lonely

Talk to me I ask

I should learn not to ask

For more than you give me.

I long for more

It's nature

To want to satisfy wants

Not have this battle going on

While we are touching.

FORGIVENESS

We haven't spoken for years

There was no fight

We came to this unspoken agreement

We stopped talking to each other

Why not?

There was no love

Lots of envy

For the different things we had

Slowly dividing us.

We grew old

Neither knowing our

Pets, spouse, or kids.

Such a loss

For a family that once knew fun

At breakfast, at dinner, and in the backyard

This still warm morning

I mourn for the loss

As if I mourn the dead

I silently beg for forgiveness

No one will hear.

MY SON THE ADDICT

He lies

He steals

He manipulates

He finally

Tells all

Swears it is the truth

Promises never to

Engage

Lie

Steal, again

Yet, the pain remains

Tomorrow will speak for itself

Change has a habit of moving

Slowly or

Not at all.

BETRAYAL

You're never the same

Nor is the relationship

Try to keep the status quo

For the relationship

Yet pain lingers within the soul

Stain of black on the white

Bride's dress

Black, stinky and sticky

Could not wash the stain out

You walk around with the stain

Hoping no one

Can see, feel, smell

The mess

Betrayal brought.

Intriguing how you come in late
I think it's nothing
It's repeated
Week after week
To think I let it go on
You really cannot believe
One can betray without care
When love is the bridge
Between two.
Cheating became routine
Heartache became routine
Take the damn dress off.

TONIGHT, THE MOUTH IS SHUT

Cannot fight another night

If I do not speak

There is no cause

For the fight

Silence stops the fight

Silence stops the love;

Even this takes courage.

A wounded bird

With clipped wings

Has more life than I

Weak to the core

So weak blood

Cannot flow

Nor can the heart beat.

A SILENT COMPLAINER

Yet, I can hear

Those complaints

Loud and clear.

I CRIED

When you did not

Leave

Your betrayal

Was the voice

I hoped you would leave

When I found out.

Instead, you said

I am sorry, so sorry

I accepted

With tears

What a night

What a high

Attempting to love in pain

For I was too weak to leave

I cried for I was

Too weak to leave.

GRANDMA

Stay out of it

I know

Better yet

I knew you would not like my

Tattoos.

I wanted one

So I got one

Now I have four.

The worst tattoo

One name of the boy you didn't

Like

His name in bold letters

You told me he was too controlling.

He told me, if you love me

You will place my name near your

Heart

So, I did to prove I loved him.

Stupid

Now I want to ask you

Can you help me pay

To remove his name

Upon my heart

In very bold letters?

NO IMPACT

Over my child

Tomorrow, he turns eighteen

He will walk out the door

He tells me

Never wants to talk to

Me again.

I know what I have done

To cause all this

I have apologized

Over and over.

He said he hates me and

Tonight is

Our last argument

Our last talk

For he does not believe

I will be

The mom he wants.

Sometimes there

Is a weakness within

No matter how much I wanted

I could not change

Nor could he.

IF YOU DO NOT KEEP ME

I will break

I want to say

To the man that promised me

To love, cherish

Be faithful

Care for me when ill.

Now you give me wounds within

You keep up

A good show for

All our friends

I remember all

The vows tonight

While sitting in a chair

Beside the front window

Waiting

In the middle of the night

For your return.

LAST NIGHT

Fell in love

The kind that is

Head over heels in love

This morning

The love is in mourning

Getting ready to let go

Love misunderstood

Certainly not love anymore

Although the smell of love

Is ever present

As I gather my clothes,

Ashamed.

UPSET

I ask

Why are you so bitter?

My love

Has turned into a battlefield

Cannons going off

With the look of hate

So much time and energy

Lost

Time is all I have

You used too much

Unable to hide

The hate

The bitterness

I lie in darkness

Wanting to hold on

Knowing you're on your way out.

KEEPSAKES

I have so many things I saved

I knew one day

I would be looking at all the souvenirs

Of our relationship

She left.

But these things remain

I have

Tickets to our first concert

We went to see Paul McCartney

I spent seven-hundred dollars for those tickets

That at least should have

Kept her close for a few weeks

No, she left three days after the concert.

I have the poem I wrote

Which I will not share with her now

I have the hankie she returned.

I gave it to her when her period started

While sitting in my car watching the moon rise

I even have the photo we took of sunrise

By the sea.

She left me wanting more kisses

Upon my cheeks

One more cooked meal

I know it's an old story

Yet I loved her cooking

Loved hugging her while she stood

By the warm stove

(continued)

Felt like we were going to make it

For a lot longer than we did.

At night the treat of talking

Holding each other, laughing

About how we acted as kids

Until dawn

Now, I have the leftover

Love that is a dream

No, the nightmare.

Oh, never again to have her

Answer my kisses

No response is overwhelming

Pain.

LIKE LOVE

Suffering is always going on

These two are always

Written about

Talked about

Sung about

They are in paintings

Books written and

Movies made.

Pondered by parents

Of how their kids

Will meet up

With love and suffering.

Icarus with his waxed wings

Loved the idea of

Flying, so he did and

Suffered

As he fell fast

To the sea

For all to hear

His fall.

Love brought on his suffering

For love must run its course.

I EAT FOR A REASON

Not only to get fat

I eat to hide the pain

Life dishes out

We all get a little

Here and there

We just have to live through the pain.

For most of us

It passes

The outliers of pain

The pain that gives you the

Energy to eat to get fat

The pain you think about

Each night

The pain that wakes you

In the middle of the night.

The pain that hits your

Thoughts first thing in the morning

I eat for

The pain that remains.

UNFORGIVING

People do bad things

I have a hard time

Forgiving

The pain

Caused

For they leave

You in the

Snotty puddle of tears.

SHOOK BY DRIVE-BY

Seeing you riding by

In your Porsche

Opening wounds

That are yet to heal

Remembering intimacy now lost.

Could not have planned

The pain that arrives by chance

You still consume my thoughts

Every nightmare turns into cries.

The hardship comes when nightmares

Must be navigated in the daylight

Repeated hurts

Rain or shine

Understand his new desires

While mine remain the same.

A deep breath

Brings a second of comfort`

Then, embrace life after

The bitter split.

HOW DO YOU KNOW

When it's time

To quit?

A feeling

A slap in the face

A lie.

SILENT

Falling sunset

Days end

Quieting my mind

Mending my soul.

WE THOUGHT

She had to figure out

The way out

Of her

Screwed-up life.

With a caring heart

That is suffering in pain

She relied on

Cats, dogs, birds, and squirrels

For love.

Long ignored by her family

She walked away

To live with

The homeless.

Learned to allow

Dirt to build

Upon her skin

Now, we pay attention

It's easy to agonize

Look for forgiveness

When we do not know

Her whereabouts.

ALCOHOL

Mom, you did

Say I do not love you

I do not want to be your mom

That's what I heard

That's what I remember.

You made promises

That were never kept

You did silly things

To cover up your

Drinking.

It made me sick when

The scent of alcohol

Was in the air

Especially hated the smell

When I came home from school.

I wanted to talk with you

Share my day with you

You were broken

You then broke me

Understanding who you were

I fear being with you

Now that I am on my own

I want to keep it that way

Unable to forgive for

Fear

Of remembering

What I need to forget.

DID NOT GET ONE

The warm fuzzy

Mom

The one that bakes warm cookies on a cold night

Dinners you are happy to share with friends

Instead, there is the one I got.

Somehow, I survived

The bitch

The drunk

The slob

The mom who was not around when I came

Home from school.

Once I asked my sister

Is she dead?

So still

Lying on the floor

As a matter of fact, my sister

Answered

No, she is drunk.

I learned to fend for myself

I took money from Mom's purse

Went to the store

Cooked dinner for all of us

Very intricate dishes

Tuna fish sandwiches

With a side of baked beans

Glad we had a can opener

I put dinner on the table.

Thanks, Campbell soup

For the recipe on the soup cans

Inexpensive and easy to follow

Meatloaf was my favorite

So many different things you can put in meatloaf

Always tasted pretty good.

Few dishes and pots needed

Plus, I loved squeezing the

Hamburger meat through my fingers

I was so hungry while cooking

I loved to eat the raw meat.

There was no choice

You can whine

You can cry

You can be mean

Stay at friends' homes

I wanted to do better

Be better

I figured out how to deal with

A drunk.

WHAT IS THIS BURDEN

Overlooking my shoulder

On my life's journey

Weighing me down

That I cannot speak

Of what I feel

It is an injustice

To our marriage

More important

Injustice to me

What a fool to have loved more

To the one who

Can put his hate before his love.

ENOUGH

When is enough, enough?

My brother said that to my sister

She was taking money from Mom

For her care and transportation

He was upset

I heard him say

When is enough, enough?

He was hurt

I was too

Mom in between

Two kids she loved.

The tiny joys received from a sibling's love

Tangled up in the burden of care

Tough job, caring for the elderly.

Help at her convenience and need

Her role as caregiver was twenty-four-seven

Something taken from each

Sister's time, brother's money

Mom caught

Needing care

Mom worried of losing one's love.

ARRIVAL

Death is on the way

Knowing started with

Eternal melancholy

Wondering, is this the last time

Of everything and anything?

Thinking swings from

The way it was to the way it is

Vagueness encompasses all

Emotions, for I know death is coming.

I really do not want its visit

We had a great time

Until death came knocking

There is the constant

Pit in my stomach

I wake with it

I dream with it

This bodily pain

As real as any broken bone.

This night

We held each other

As tightly as two can

Before the day, our time ends.

THE PERFECT ALIGNMENT

From life to death

At your own hand

The killing of self

When the battle of life

Gets too hard for us.

Most days we recover

We see the clearing of the skies

Feel the warm sun upon our face

We get through the current crisis

The tug of war ends for the day

Then there is the day

The one day where

It's the storm that does not subside

Where there is no light

It's the darkest of days

The coldest of nights.

Morning too far away

The time slowly moving

Worse yet, at a standstill

The perfect alignment

Surrendering

To end the will for life.

TRASH

It's garbage day

I empty all the small cans

Around the house

Not a big job except for the kitchen.

This morning

I see a piece of paper in my husband's garbage can

Not his writing

I focus and do the worst thing I could

I pick up the paper and read

It's a letter from what I guess is a wannabe

Lover for him.

She writes about how hard it is when he calls her

By my name

Well that's good, one point for me

How long will it take you to make a choice, her or me?

Point two for me

He does not want to leave

Maybe none of this is point-driven

He might just want a bit of fun

A little adventure

The excitement of sneaking around

Learning he can

Not change his life at all

Why did he throw this single piece of paper

In the garbage, knowing full well I'd be there?

Did he want to get caught?

Did he want me to fight for him?

Did he want me to leave him?

Now I think I married a coward

Someone else has to decide

His life for him

His wife

Or

His girlfriend.

DARKNESS

Brought no comfort

As if darkness has

Any room for comfort

SPEAKING

To you way too many times

You are listening, I know for sure

Just no comments.

I can still smell you on your clothes

You left with me to take care of

At night, your smell is the strongest

On your pillows.

This leads to what I miss the most

It is your arms

The warmth they gave me

Through the forty-five years we spent together.

I am sorry for my loss

Extraordinary, how I know

You're out there

Feeling the loss of me.

ANNOYANCES

It has started

I no longer like the noises he makes when sleeping

I no longer like the noises he makes when eating

I no longer like how fast he eats

I no longer like the way he corrects everyone.

I no longer like that he openly kisses me once a day

I no longer like that he goes to his mom's house

First, then home

I no longer like that he will not pick up a dead roach

On the floor.

I no longer like when I make a request, he says no

Without even thinking

I no longer like that he pretends not to hear me

When speaking

I no longer like that he changes channels and
Watches nothing
Just clicks away.
I no longer like that he puts music on when
I am sitting quietly in a room
I no longer like being in the same room.
I left yesterday, annoyances stopped
I wrote down the annoyances
I no longer care, people asking why I left
Now I know what to say
To snoopy friends who ask
Why did you leave?

STUNNED

Helping a loved one

With addiction

Never thought I would be the one

Not a book or lesson or sermon

Prepared me to help

The addict I love.

Get up off the floor,

Wipe the vomit off your face

Hope, pray this will be the last time

I have to pick up the drunk.

What I do hasn't helped

Three years of questioning

Is he addicted or just drinking too much?

Am I just imagining

If I help today

Will it be the last?

How do I get help?

Do I walk away?

That's really what I want

If there was love

It's turned into deadweight chaos.

GIFT FROM GOD

Some days I question the

Absence of God and His creation.

Why would He do such a magnificent job

The sun, the moon, singing birds

Then forget Anthony?

My five-year-old, suffering

The inoperable tumor in his head

In pain, disoriented, alone in bed most days

Waiting for death without understanding

How

Easily a light goes out.

IT IS DEATH

That brought me to this closet

I study the clothes hanging so

Neatly

One inch apart, ironed with perfection

I want to wear one or two

To feel his touch again

Through his clean, perfectly ironed shirts

Knowing this borrowed item

Will ease my sorrow.

SUNRISE CALLS TO ME

No matter how lonely

I am

To let me know

I belong

SPEAK LOUD

Give into courage

Suffer the silence no longer

Begone eyes of tears

Walk tall, trust self

Speak to win for self

Allow your mind

Allow your heart

Allow your soul

To love.

MY LOVE

So much like a bee

Roaming from one flower

To the next flower

Busy bee removing

The sweetness of life

From each flower visited

Leaving

The lonely flower

Wasted

IT IS DONE AND OVER

That is the path of forgiveness

I could scream about your behavior

For days on end

Only to raise the depth of my hurt.

I say you are forgiven

I love you

In ease of my pain

For I know you are void of pain

You little shit.

I decided not to let you know

Where I stand, and how I feel

Repercussions for me will

Arrive, in the middle of the night.

SCENT OF SMOKE REMAINS

As the fire of love smelters

Into thin air, within high winds

Creating the storm of loss

CHASTITY

Belts were good ideas
Play all you want
It is just a roaming finger
No destroying the wealth

Where is today's door?
There is no stopping
Feels too good to stop
Vulnerability on fire
Done without gentleness
Done without skill

It has gone as fast as a lost dream
We are now equal
Virginity, no high order
We worry more about the use of sunscreen
The real dream gone
So young.

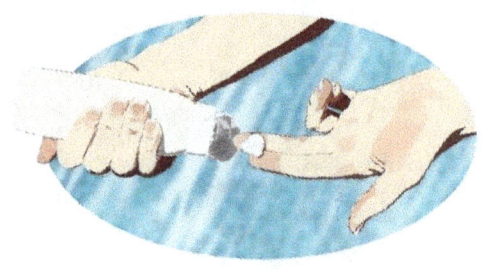

ONCE WE WERE THOUGHT OF AS US

Now weak and lean

That you're gone

You left in the rain

As flowers bloomed

From nighttime rain

Warmed by the

Morning sun.

Night is over

Rain has gone

As the darkest

Of nights

Pass with

Fear

I settle for

Dreaming.

YOU'RE MARRIED

You should be a happy bride and groom

You found the one

The one you look at with adoring eyes

For me I know

I will never be one with you

Nor hear your footsteps

As they came to my bed

Never, never, never

Again.

THE STRENGTH OF TWO

By moonlight

What's going to happen when the sun rises

Along with the multitudes of people

Who rise early as the sun?

Secure and warm in your arms

What's going to happen when the sun rises

Will you return by moonlight?

What's going to happen when the sun rises

I really know;

You will not return by moonlight.

MY WIFE WAS NEVER INTERESTED IN BEING FAITHFUL

I knew this before I married her

Thinking getting married

Being committed

Would change her thought of how hard I worked for

Us.

Three months I have to repeat this

Three months

Such a short time

For her to start looking for another

She signed up for a dating service

I found out.

I signed up on the same dating service

Strange, next Tuesday I have

A tentative meeting at a Starbucks

Thirty-four miles from our home

With my wife.

I am not going to show up

I will let her waste time driving to meet

The new lover "me"

I will play hard to get this time.

SHE SAID I LOVE YOU

Seven times today

My heart tells me

Either she wants to know I love her too

Or she really does not love me

Yet, is trying to convince herself.

Worst thing about this is

I know I do not love her

Too insecure and bossy for me to love.

Time to start looking for another

Today

I said that seven times to myself.

HAUNTED

The battlefields

Must be haunted

Every single one of them

To tell the tales of horror

At the graves of our slain

For so many are strangers

To each other

They had better not be lonely

Giving

Up life, to do battle

Vast battlefields

Still not quiet.

STUPID

Love gave growth to being a porter
Carrying everything it takes to stay
All the risks, responsibilities, and time
Become the garbage collector of staying.

YOUNG BOY LOVED HIS GRANDMOTHER

Grieves among photos he has collected through the years

Of get-togethers

They are cherished possessions

Not to be burned

When he dies.

Can anyone understand his love for an old lady?

The comfort she bought to his life

Photos remind him of his loss

The good times gone

He is determined not to forget

He wants her memory to be forever.

He cries

He longs

His grief is gentle

Mad at the way

The world works

Glad for the time

Within a

Graceful life until death.

ISOLATION

Living by oneself

Has grown on me

No one tells me to do anything

Yet, I am hurting.

I have no one to fight with

I get to think

Quickly

Quietly

On my own time.

I can place a book

Open on my nightstand

No one touches it

No complaints

Yet, I am hurting.

I can watch TV at two a.m.

I can go on social media

Anytime night or day

Find someone somewhere

To chat with

No complaints

Yet, I am hurting.

No disruptions before I

Finish my hot morning coffee

I have become

The man-in-waiting

For

Hugs, kisses, and holding hands

I am hurting.

HER FORGIVENESS

We are still together

Yet I know she often thinks

Why did I betray her?

Not sure I know either

I regret what I did

She has taken me back

We forged ahead

Fourteen years have gone by

I still cannot forgive myself

Knowingly hurting someone

I love.

Wonder, does she think of this as often

As I?

Pretty sure

Taking me back is her forgiveness

What I really like

She has never once talked about it

Never once thrown it back in my face

She is kind, loving, caring.

Glad I get to hold her tonight

No precise way to know

How to forgive myself

Unforgiveness has cold days.

TEENAGER AT RISK

His intricate developing mind
Frozen at thirteen maybe twelve
That's the age it started
His first swig of vodka
The brand unknown.
It's the bottle that's open
Difficult to detect usage
Displayed on Dad's bar
All sorts of drinks
He chose vodka.
The strange rapport begins
Teen and vodka.
Soon to cheat on vodka
With whatever is around that
Works.
Accepts each new brand with love
It all takes him away from life
The goals of tomorrow undeveloped
Stops him from

Becoming an adult.

Brain gone to sleep

Possibility for good

A life hard remembered, he is

Never to age in mind.

Compassion for the

Teenager at risk

Slowly dissipates

At sunrise

The sun, hot and shining

I think

Of what might have been.

Lost in body

The teenager

Who loved wild

Never to say no

To a swig

Cheapest of vodka

Or anything that's available

Missed by me, his mom.

GRANDDAUGHTER NOT HAVING FUN

Fun is what I want the most for this seven-year-old

She is alone

Mother and dad went their way

Grandma is the caretaker

Not a new mom

For parents come and go

As the court gives them time

To visit.

They have rights

I have to supervise

They have rights

My granddaughter has to suffer

With their rights

I have to waste time supervising.

Granddaughter has to deal with

Grief of a new life

I'm old

Tired most days

Can you imagine falling asleep

At ten each night?

The time my granddaughter wants

To tell me about her day

Do my best

I try naps and coffee at five just to fight

The dozing off.

Parents have to see granddaughter at the

Court-appointed time

If they do not show, they cannot come by at their leisure

I teach cooking and sewing to kids

In the neighborhood.

She does smile

Now and then

My delight

Her right

As a kid.

LETTING MYSELF DIE

Woke up

Not caring

Not wanting

Didn't want to get dressed

Stopped my writing

Stopped my reading

Just sat all day

In a chair.

Wanted to even pee

In my pants

No calls outgoing

Better yet, no incoming calls

Answered to no one;

Silent all day.

No dreams of tomorrow

Only the past filled with

Regrets.

An old lady

Wrote, if I

Could do it all over again

I would have less regrets

Or did she write more regrets?

That's all I have, is regrets

How can one get it

So very wrong?

IT SEEMS WE HURRY LOVE

As if we are about to cease

Time running out

No matter what, get this thing

Called love going

Which leads one to do

Stupid things.

Like, if in the first three dates

You do not like what's going on

You keep dating

As if you had the power to change others

The one that loves more, is the one

That will change as quickly and quietly

As your garden chameleon.

THIS MOMENTARY PLEASURE

Of sleeping with Ralph

Took my soul.

Now

Weakened and alone

I would like to know

Why

I would do it all over again

Which

Gives me the understanding

There is no cure for stupid.

MISTAKES ARE MADE

By all of us

These mistakes

Fill us with regrets

We wonder how

Could I have been so stupid

By now, you have found out

Stupid is hard to fix

The one mistake to avoid

Is who you choose for your

Life partner

It is a life sentence

Your partner is

Interlaced with every aspect of

Your life.

If you have chosen poorly

Let life be long enough

Keep in mind the statement

Until death do us part

Let us not make

The same mistake for

Eternity.

BEFORE YOU LEAVE

Hold my hand

I am beginning to miss

The comfort your hand

Holds for me

ALWAYS

That's the thought

When I decided to marry

Wanted to be there for you

Wanted you to be there for me

We took vows with

Family, friends, parents

As witness to our love.

Such a spectacular event

You were the most beautiful person

Loved your smile

Your embrace

Three months into the marriage

I encountered competition

Unreal

Cheated, when I loved you the most

Yes, I have to repeat

When I loved you the most

I thought we would be forever.

Now, lonely nights

Lonely days

In the dark, both day and night

Took away hope

Questioned love

Took off the band of gold

You never wore one

I should have known

Yet, I could not see

It was impossible to look away from

The love I imagined

Darkened life arrived.

Two things I am glad of

I was not a virgin

Nor were any kids on the way

Just me, to endure.

THE ESSENCE OF LONGING

Being in love

Never stops the longing

Longing hangs around your beating heart

No one can be all you want

Choose wisely

Treat with kindness

Get the best of what you need

To feel loved

To love

Let some of what you choose

Be good enough

To stop the longing.

THE PURPLE BRUISE

Shows up

Days after

The blow

Yet remembered

The day of the blow.

AT DEATH

You need to know

Maybe we all know

It's life out

As quick as one turns off

The light switch

At night.

I suppose it's dark and

Quiet

Although I have heard

From those that have had

Near end-of-life experiences

There is a bright light

To guide and welcome you

With a sense of peace and

No more fight

We are ready for the next journey

Then the concern arises

How do I take care of my

Love's memory?

I want to follow the

Rituals we had

Wanting the memory of our life together

To last as long as our favorite song.

I WANTED SOLITUDE

Talked myself into solitude as needed

I am alone now

I see something I want to tell someone

I cannot

I am alone.

Happiness needs to be shared

Solitude turns into loneliness

As if it's a gentle wave of a wicked witch's wand.

I WANT TO DANCE

Until my feet ache

Under the full moon

Warming the air between us

Splendor not to be mine

Nor yours

Such, such fools

To forgo the joy

Not to join in the dance

The fool in me stays only

As a fool can do

Without a clear mind

Telling myself stick around

The dance

Not really wanted.

WROTE A LETTER TO MOM

She is not here

Yet I want her to

Have the letter.

Letters are of the past

So much meaning

More than a text.

Letters let you feel

The person writing

You can have time to reread

The letter anytime.

I place the letter

In an envelope

Tack it to the tree

Mom sat under

Many hot days

Watching us

Play.

I know when she has time

Mom will read my letter

I await her hug in a real dream.

NEED TO SEPARATE

I now know she is not good for me

I have tried

Flowers

Rubbing her back

Letting her know how pretty she is

I say I love you

Each morning.

I think

What can I do to brighten her day

There is no return

I feel unloved

Even though I love.

I think of all the millions

Of cells we have in our body

Separating by the second

Do they agonize over

Their separation

As I am

Or do they just do it

Because that's what you do

To live.

SHE AND I ARE IN LOVE

We tell the world

We tell ourselves

Truth for me is she loves me

In parts.

There are things about me she loves

I care

She loves being cared for

She does not love the part of me

That has little ambition

I'm content with making sure

She has what she needs.

I get up and get her a drink

Of her choosing

Right when the movie is

At the junction of

You got to see this.

Let us replay this scene

She loves the part of me that feels her pain

She loves the part of me that can

Dance in front of the world

Girls want to line up for a spin with me

She hates the part of me that

Likes to make sure all is done

Before I turn out the lights.

She overwhelms me

She loves that she overwhelms me

I am happy to get the parts she gives

It's not the love of perfection

It is the love that will do

In parts.

WEEPING

While I was

Waiting for the bus

The rain came down

No raincoat

No umbrella

Not even a tissue

Not a soul concerned

Way too immersed in hurriedness

Life's relentlessness brings

To each of us daily battles.

GOODBYE MY LOVE

Watching your spirit

Leave

As tender the moment

Horror shapes the mood

More than I wanted

To ever experience.

Death expected

Hard felt loss hushed by defeat

As if death never happened

Before

Your death.

HE HAS GROWN COLD

For life was taken

Loss of heat traveled this path

I sit in stillness

Know life was lost;

My brother's life.

His significance was of little

Importance to most

To me, he gave strength

Brought laughter with his breath

My calls always answered

Now never to be answered

Unless I pretend

Which will be between me and

What allows me to dream.

My loss now realized

With the onset of darkness

For who I love

Will

Never be again.

ONGOING ADVERSITY

Much going against

This little girl

Stress, troubles, hurdles

This heart-wrenching life

One has to overcome

To become a woman.

I watch with guilt and grief

Her hammered by her

Abuser

I stop the watching

Begin the help

Confident I can make a difference.

This world we call

Civilized, has

No answer

She stays with her parents

This little girl wants to stay.

Now I know

What kids do for love.

SHOW ME

You are listening

I can never tell

For your comments

Have nothing to do

With what I have said.

TALKING BACKWARDS

Every morning, I make breakfast

I start with hot tea

While I have my tea, I read the newspaper

Do a puzzle

It's a great ritual for me.

Then the issue starts

Hubby comes

He loves my cooking

I do too

We have it all

Eggs, bacon, pancakes, toast, rolls

Muffins, the list goes on

Love the ritual until we sit to eat.

He starts talking about

Things that happened thirteen years ago

This morning, he says

I wish I had gone to college with Jake

(Our son)

If I had helped settle him in

He would have done better.

It's every morning

Every possible regret

So tired today

I felt like taking the frying pan to

Hit him over the head

Not once, at least twice

More, if needed to release my anger.

Now I have to find a new ritual

There is no way I'm going to jail

No breakfast

I go walking instead

To the nearest Starbucks.

He shifts for himself

He talks to himself

He seems satisfied

I know I am;

I listen to the words of nature

Which has no regrets.

WE HAVE GROWN OLD

Together with our dreams

Fulfilled

Blessed

Now our life has passed

A bit bitter

Unable

To lengthen

Our journey.

YEARS AGO

Thanksgiving dinner

At my home

Included twenty-one people

Yesterday, we only had

Eleven

Yes, eleven.

The others have gone

They died

Yes, death was noticed

At Thanksgiving.

I should be thankful I knew them

I laughed with them

We shared love with them

They are remembered

Uncle Pete

Uncle Sam

Aunt Juanita

Mom

Dad

Brother John

John

Jeff

Gene

Uncle Nick

Yes, remembered while

I set the table for fewer.

LOVE TOGETHER

We place our hearts

In each other's hands

With a delight as fresh as

The slice of watermelon

On a warm summer's day.

Time has given us our dream

To make us who we are

Our hearts beat in rhythm

As we weep with joy

Today

In communion of love

Yet

Seized by fear

Knowing

All love ends.

HE IS DEAD

He was a terrible husband

Yeah I know, a good father

Even with his faults, I stayed with him

I hate the fact I stayed

Was staying in place for the kids

Was it more economical?

I did not have the balls to leave.

Now I miss his gentle

Touch upon my forehead

Before I fell into a deep sleep

For I felt safe next to him

The only sign of affection shown.

As I tell you this, I feel the pain

A life without my husband

Who I decided to stay with

For reasons that seem

Reasonable today.

MARRIED THIRTY-SEVEN YEARS

This morning I thought

Why did it take so long

For me to realize how

Important you are to me?

How much I love you

How much I enjoy our hugs

How much I feel her growing old

Even as we age

Wanting you, more than yesterday

My indulgence.

LOVE CORRODED

No one did anything

It happened

The smile when she

Entered a room is gone

Barely notices I am waiting

For the smile

That warms my heart.

We became detached

Effort was too time-consuming

Really not wanted

Accepting the coolness of love.

We do hold hands

We do hug

We do kiss on the cheek

For a hello and goodbye.

Something is still going on

It's just not the heavy

Exciting love that meant

We wanted to touch all day long

The sparkle after a day apart

There is something

It's leftovers.

SMART CRAZY

Or is it crazy smart?

I dated a guy, brilliant

But crazy

Head of his class

Bottom of the list

With relationships

Guy.

No friends, he said

While I'm on a date with him

Hello, I am someone.

Maybe that's the reason you have

No friends

You think everyone is a no one.

I had to stop seeing him

I thought he just might

Beat me.

He hated people

Always found the wrong

No one was good enough

All I wanted, was romance

A fun date

Instead, I learned every

Bad thing about being me.

Before the date

I truly was happy with myself

No quick fix with him

It was just up to me

To never answer his phone calls.

MORNING SADNESS WAKES ONE

The deed that carried your love away

Like a fleeting hurricane

Quick to destroy, quick to leave

Pick up the pieces of destruction

Joy lost in the wind.

As the days melt together

The rain comes

Bringing comfort in its rhythm

Survived a few days that seem like

Forever

Sadness from love.

Wonder, do I love again?

For any and all love ends in sadness.

LISTEN

You act as if you haven't heard

Did you hear?

Did you care?

He has died

Yes, death came

Listen to my sadness

Not worry about how long

Winter will last this year

Listen to my sadness

His death came.

MY UNHEARD STORY

Will be buried in dirt

There are so many

Like me

That have and will not

Have their story heard

No matter how we scream

Our story will be left untold

Silent, forgotten, and invisible.

THIS IS LOVE

How it makes me weary

Leaves me wanting

Unsatisfied

Cries unheard, unfelt as they

Drift in the wind.

Once I thought love to be

Rewarding and uplifting

A place where angels go

How weary this love

Why bother?

I watch the sunrise

Feel its warmth

While the sun heals my weary heart.

ONE MORE

Tear over a broken heart

One more

Song about a broken heart

One more

Poem about a broken heart

This one is easy, it's my broken heart

Never will I be over this.

Friends remind me

Of the hurt you brought on

Just because you could

When you wanted it over

You went about

The breakup with ease

Dreams became nightmares.

I think about how I loved you more

Each day when together

How did I not know?

Where was my brain?

This was the love

That became my nightmares.

When I first started dreaming of you

The dreams were filled with the joy

Of wonder

I saw trees in full bloom, the greenest of leaves

The one embedded on my brain

With our initials carved inside a heart

I saw sunny, clear blue skies

Thinking again

Of our time together.

Now

When I meet you on the street

Do I walk on by or

Spit to aim for your lips?

Yet

All I want to do

Is run into your arms

The damn fool am I.

EACH MONTH

At first weekend

Jimmy goes to the cemetery

To visit all his relatives

That have passed away

He puts a sunflower

On their grave.

As he ages, he worries

Who will bring them

A bit of sunshine

When he is not here?

He buys the biggest bag

Of sunflower seeds

Plants them all around the graves.

Just maybe they will bloom

For him and

All his loved ones.

I FELL IN LOVE

Now I want to be better

Each day

For my love

Harder than I thought

I can do this

I want to do this

For I want to be the one

That loves more.

SHY OF FORECAST

After the first week or so

We want forever

It's easier to forecast

Tomorrows together

We look for ways to

Raise the heat with sunny days.

When we want

Each other's response to love

We offer a bit more

Of ourselves.

We stay the course

Even if forecast is cloudy

Rather than change

We go for sub-zero

Fear of change

Expect no sunny days

Expect no return on time

Forecast modest love.

I RECRUITED

Myself

To write.

Write about the hurt

The pain I have

Experienced

Understanding

Weakness, not

To fight.

Fatigue set in

The fight was lost

On every front.

So, I live through

Poems that do

Not rhyme

Do not have any rules

Just write the thoughts

That come floating in, to

Ease the pain and

Reduce regrets.

ABSENCE OF WONDER

No events today

Weary with each step I take

For love has left

As if I have thrown a rock into the sea

Never to be seen again

Dropped to the floor

With such speed

Out of sight.

Leaves a memory to fade as the ripples fade

So my heart stops pounding

My eyes stop searching

The sea moves

The day ends

Weary am I.

WRONGED BY LOVE

In the dark of winter

Love melted in the soft, cold snow

There I lay

In the soft, cold snow

Wanting what I lost

Heart once excited

Now understands

How easily love melts.

Love, pure as the newly fallen snow

Now

Impaired

In the soft, cold snow

That's soon to melt

Revealing the dirt

Hurt brings.

SADNESS

Without a desire to be

Of good cheer

Just to think if I can only

Move up to melancholy

This heart of mine

Has sunk to new lows.

Not just one item

A multiple of thoughts

In a perfectly straight line

Finishing at sadness.

Unhappiness joins a

Spirit so low, sobbing

Hour to hour

Weeping alone.

ANONYMITY

That's what I want

Life has been so very hard

I will feel better if no one knows

My quiet tears.

NO BATTLE TODAY

I can no

Longer sink into battle

With the one I love

For neither of us

Can be kind to each other

Our mood distrusting

Who we became.

PROTECTION

From abuse

Ruins you

For you isolate

Hide and

Try

Not to care

About the sadness of abuse.

IT'S A LOSS

I do not have our love right

Yet, if I could love you more

I would not be me

There is no way

For me to love you

Less

For my heart would not

Allow a halfway love.

EMERGENCY

That's what I want

Life has been so very hard

The two in the morning call

Rushing to the hospital

She is sick again

For twenty-six years

Battling cancer

Her body has been

Blasted with drugs

Due to cancer, with

All its side effects.

She is here again

I hold her hand

She looks into my eyes, says

I can't do this anymore.

I tell her, you do not have

To make that choice now

It is yours whenever you're ready.

Three days later I am picking

Her up to go home

Was not as bad as I thought, she says

I am happy

She is better and going home.

Sunday is her grandson's

Fourth birthday

Luckily, she bought his present

The red wagon for all his toys.

Yes, she has asked her

Body

One more

Birthday please.

I WATCHED OTHERS

Thinking how they enjoy their love

Is love as good as it

Looks from a distance?

Watching the hand-holding

The laughter by lovers

Does love have as many issues

As loneliness?

Sour are my thoughts for

At times I think love can bring

On a greater loneliness than

Being alone.

LOVE'S HIGH STAKE

For each of us

For there is danger

Indignities given

By persons

Who enjoy

Stepping on one's soul

Just because they can.

WHILE I CRY

The world goes on

I cried

You went on

MY LOSS

More than I thought it would affect me

She has died

Three years later I still miss her

Question my grief

People who know me want me to move on

That's such a cruel thought

Moving on when you're not ready.

STUPIDITY

All my crying equals stupidity

To start with, there is

There was

Not enough loving

Simple.

The night my heart died

Thinking we can make it

Now realizing, I am all

By myself

Our world left behind

By you

Belongs to me

Alone

The night my heart died

With plenty of time for crying.

To think

I let you whisper in my ear

Sweet nothings

Thinking the words had meaning

You ask

Do you still love him

Yes, I answer

Started with stupidity

Ending with stupidity.

BITTERSWEET

I have always loved dancing

My husband hates it

Not sure why he hates it

It's something he would rather not do

He thinks everyone is watching him

I want everyone to watch

In the arms of my man

Today he dances with me

Each night he dances with me

Sometimes early in the morning

Dance

For now, sleep is difficult

What a change

I wonder if the growing tumor

Has anything to do with it?

It is okay

I still want to dance

Especially with my man

Even though I am bald, weak, dizzy

Bittersweet, yes

Yet

Getting something longed for.

I WANT TO CALL IT A THING

Love

So much attached

To this thing I call love

I often think love has no feelings

Lots of times it has no loyalty

It is like an itch that needs scratching

As if that will answer all needs.

For the want I have, to be love, to

Feel the warmth of closeness love brings

Yet, I have known the love

That grows hate when love is wrong.

It's important

It's imperative

I shout for love and there is no response

All the thoughts and emotions that come

    With this thing I call love

    There is hope in love, yet

        Love always ends

        In sadness.

    Disappointment in love

    Which calls us to solitude.

When love is right, its want is

        Forever and

        Then some.

WEPT

My mother wept

Until she wept

Without tears

For years

Conceivably

Centuries

Mothers

Have wept

To protect

To nourish

To love

To teach

The scope of

What mothers do

Invisible even to the

Eyes of angles

EVERY TIME

I see her

She triggers

A pain within

I had to rid myself

Of the desire for her.

Once I tabled desire

I released myself from

Competing with pain

There was the lesson.

Pain was part of the desire

To triumph over this

Addiction of pain

I called love.

GO FORWARD

DO NOT FEAR A BROKEN HEART

FOR THE WANT OF LOVE

NEVER DIES

www.ingramcontent.com/pod-product-compliance
Lightning Source LLC
Chambersburg PA
CBHW050248010526
44107CB00003B/232